Kip and the Vet

By Carmel Reilly

Vic got her vet bag.

Vic got in her van
to go and see Kip.

Kip sat on his dog bed.

"Look, Vic!" said Val.
"Kip can not get up
for a run."

Val got a rug.

"Sit on my lap, Kip,"
said Val.

Kip sat up.

Kip got off Val's lap.

Wag, wag!

Kip ran and ran ...
and ran!

CHECKING FOR MEANING

1. How did Vic get to Val's house? *(Literal)*

2. What did Kip do when he got off Val's lap? *(Literal)*

3. Why do you think Val got a rug for Kip to sit on? *(Inferential)*

EXTENDING VOCABULARY

Val's	Look at the word *Val's*. What is the base of this word? What has been added to the base? How does adding an apostrophe and an *s* change the meaning of the word?
This	What two letters make the first sound in the word *This*? Find another word in the book that starts with the same letter–sound pattern.
van	A *van* is a medium-sized vehicle, often used for delivering goods. What other types of vehicles can you name?

MOVING BEYOND THE TEXT

1. What sort of bug might have bitten Kip?

2. Have you ever been bitten by a bug? What sort of bug was it?

3. What are some other animals that vets take care of?

4. What do you think Vic might have in her vet bag?

SPEED SOUNDS

Kk	Ll	Vv	Qq	Ww
Dd	Jj	Oo	Gg	Uu

Cc	Bb	Rr	Ee	Ff	Hh	Nn
Mm	Ss	Aa	Pp	Ii	Tt	

PRACTICE WORDS

Val

Vic

Kip

vet

let

van

wag

lap

Wag